101 AMAZING FACTS ABOUT

# JACK
## THE
# RIPPER

**Jack Goldstein & Frankie Taylor**

# Contents

Introduction                         vii

The Facts                            1

Basic Facts                          1

Mary Ann Nichols                     4

Annie Chapman                        8

Elizabeth Stride                     12

Catherine Eddowes                    16

Mary Jane Kelly                      21

Letters                              26

Interesting Facts                    33

Clues to the Ripper's Identity       38

Suspects                             43

And Finally...                       51

My knife's so nice and sharp I want to get to work right away if I get a chance. Good Luck.

Yours truly

Jack the Ripper

# Introduction

It is 1888 and the foggy streets of Whitechapel, one of the poorest areas of Victorian London, are gripped by fear. Five women thought have been murdered by the same hand, all but one of their corpses terrifyingly mutilated. But who were these women? And who could the murderer be? This fascinating book contains over one hundred facts about the awful crimes of the serial killer we all know as Jack the Ripper. Organised into sections covering each individual victim, clues to the Ripper's identity, possible suspects and more, this is an excellent addition to any classic crime fan's bookshelf.

Follow Jack Goldstein on Twitter @GoldsteinBooks

Follow Frankie Taylor on Twitter @FrankieTay101

www.jackgoldsteinbooks.com

# 101 AMAZING FACTS ABOUT

# JACK THE RIPPER

# Basic Facts

1.  *Jack the Ripper* is the name given to a serial killer from late 19<sup>th</sup> century London.

2.  Not only did the Ripper kill his victims but he also mutilated their bodies.

3.  There were five 'certain' victims of Jack; all were killed in the Whitechapel area of the city between August and November of 1888.

4.  In addition to these, there were a number of later murders that it is *thought* may be connected but were never conclusively proved to have been committed by the same hands.

5.  The name 'Jack the Ripper' comes from a letter that was sent to the police claiming to be from the killer.

6.  The victims were prostitutes who lived and worked in the extremely impoverished area of London around which the killings focused.

7.  At the time, a number of factors led to Whitechapel (now in fact an affluent area) being considered a 'notorious den of immorality' – from an influx of immigration which had swelled the area's population way beyond what the amenities of the time could support to the fact there were 62 brothels and around 1200 prostitutes working in the district.

8.  We have never discovered the true identity of the killer, however there are over one hundred theories as to who he (or she) was, with a small number of 'likely' suspects.

9.  The killings spread fear and panic throughout the population of the city and led to a large-scale investigation by the Metropolitan Police.

10. Since the killings, Jack the Ripper has featured in hundreds of books (both fictional and non-fictional) as well as a huge number of movies, computer games and more.

# GHASTLY MURDER
## IN THE EAST-END.
### DREADFUL MUTILATION OF A WOMAN.

## Capture : Leather Apron

Another murder of a character even more diabolical than that perpetrated in Back's Row, on Friday week, was discovered in the same neighbourhood, on Saturday morning. At about six o'clock a woman was found lying in a back yard at the foot of a passage leading to a lodging-house in a Old Brown's Lane, Spitalfields. The house is occupied by a Mrs. Richardson, who lets it out to lodgers, and the door which admits to this passage, at the foot of which lies the yard where the body was found, is always open for the convenience of lodgers. A lodger named Davis was going down to work at the time mentioned and found the woman lying on her back close to the flight of steps leading into the yard. Her throat was cut in a fearful manner. The woman's body had been completely ripped open and the heart and other organs laying about the place, and portions of the entrails round the victim's neck. An excited crowd gathered in front of Mrs. Richardson's house and also round the mortuary in old Montague Street, whither the body was quickly conveyed. As the body lies in the rough coffin in which it has been placed in the mortuary · the same coffin in which the unfortunate Mrs. Nicholls was first placed · it presents a fearful sight. The body is that of a woman about 45 years of age. The height is exactly five feet. The complexion is fair, with wavy brown hair; the eyes are blue, and two lower teeth have been knocked out. The nose is rather large and prominent.

*Newspaper article at the time of the first murder*

# Mary Ann Nichols

11.  Mary Ann, a locksmith's daughter, was born on the 26th of August 1845 and was the first of Jack the Ripper's known murder victims.

12.  She was five feet two inches tall with brown eyes and slightly greying dark brown hair.

13.  She was an alcoholic who had not had the best lot in life. At one point she was found sleeping rough on Trafalgar Square before being placed in a workhouse. She did manage to get a job as a domestic servant, however this only lasted two months and she left, turning to prostitution as she did not get on with her employers. Earlier in her life she had married a man named William Nichols, but he had left her because of her drinking. He supported her with an allowance of five shillings a week when they split as was legally required, however the money stopped (again as law dictated) when he found out Mary Ann had turned to prostitution for additional funds. She did stay with her father for a while, but left home again after they quarrelled.

14.  She was turned away from a hostel at 18 Thrawl Street at half past one in the early hours of the 31st of August as she did not have fourpence to pay for a bed for the night. Mary Ann said she would work the street and would easily be able to earn that amount as she had acquired a new bonnet.

15. The last person to see Mary Ann alive was Nelly Holland who spoke to her at 2:30 a.m. on the corner of Osborn Street and Whitechapel Road. Mary Ann had told her she'd earned money for the night's lodgings "three times over" but had spent it all on drink.

16. Mary Ann was found at 3:40 a.m. by a cart driver called Charles Cross. She was lying on the ground, skirt raised above her waist, in front of a gated stable entrance on Buck's Row (which is today called Durward Street). Another cart driver called Robert Paul approached Cross to look at the body; Cross believed she was dead but Paul did not. After lowering her skirt to protect her modesty, the two went off to find a policeman, the closest being PC Jonas Mizen. Two further police officers – PCs John Neil and John Thain – also attended the scene.

17. She had been killed at 3:30 a.m. on the 31st of August 1888; the time of death was deduced by surgeon Dr Henry Llewellyn, who arrived at four o'clock and concluded she had died half an hour earlier.

18. The poor woman's throat had been sliced twice and her midriff had been mutilated; she had one particularly deep, jagged wound, her abdomen had also been the subject of a number of violent downward slices, as had her right hand side.

19. As there was only half a pint of blood found at the scene, Dr Llewellyn deduced that Nichols had been murdered elsewhere by the cuts to the throat which had killed her immediately. Her body had then been mutilated further (which would have taken the murderer an additional five minutes) before being dragged to the place she was found.

20. Mary Ann is buried in the City of London cemetery in a public grave with the number 210752. her resting place is marked by a plaque, placed there by the cemetery authorities in 1996.

REGISTRATION DISTRICT Whitechapel

1888. DEATH in the Sub-district of Whitechapel Church in the County of Middlesex

| No. | When and where died | Name and surname | Sex | Age | Occupation | Cause of Death | Signature, description and residence of informant | When registered | Signature of registrar |
|---|---|---|---|---|---|---|---|---|---|
| 370 | Thirty first August 1888 in the street in Bucks Row. | Mary Ann Nichols. | Female | 42 years | Wife of William Nichols Printing Machinist Walford House 35 Black street Spital fields. | Violent Syncope from Loss of blood from wounds in neck and abdomen inflicted by some sharp instrument wilfully murder by some person or persons unknown. Post Mortem. | Certificate received from Wynne E. Baxter Coroner for Middlesex Inquest held 1st & 3rd Inst & 22nd September 1888 | Twenty fifth September 1888 | John Hill Registrar |

*Death Certificate of Mary Ann Nichols*

# Annie Chapman

21. Annie, a soldier's daughter, was born Eliza Ann Smith in 1841 and was the second of Jack the Ripper's known murder victims.

22. She was five feet tall, with blue eyes and wavy dark brown hair.

23. Annie had lived a life full of tragic events. Marrying a close relative on her mother's side, John Chapman, they had three children born in 1870 (Emily Ruth), 1873 (Annie Georgina) and 1880 (John Alfred). John was born disabled and his care was handed over to a charitable school. Emily died of meningitis when she was just twelve. Finally Annie had run off with a travelling circus in the French Third Republic.

24. Because of the tragedy of effectively losing all her children, Annie and her husband had begun to drink heavily and sadly they split up. He paid her an income of ten shillings a week whilst she lived with a new partner, a man who made sieves for a living (leading to Annie's nickname 'sievey'). When the income from her husband stopped (due to his early death), Annie's partner left her and she became depressed, practically giving up on life. She moved into common lodgings, raising money from occasional crochet work and casual prostitution.

25.  At 1:45 a.m. on the 8<sup>th</sup> of September 1888, Annie was turned away from her lodgings as she did not have enough money to pay for her night's accommodation. She went out onto the streets to earn some money. The last person to see her alive was a Mrs Elizabeth Long who believes she saw Annie talking to a man wearing a deerstalker hat and long overcoat at 5:30 a.m. near to the back yard of 29 Hanbury Street in Spitalfields. The man was described as being over forty years of age, shabby but genteel and foreign in appearance and with a dark complexion.

26.  Annie's body was found at 6:00 a.m. that morning by market porter John Davis, a resident of number 29. A carpenter by the name of Albert Cadosh had entered the neighbouring yard at 5:30 a.m. and had heard voices before the sound of something weighty falling against the fence between the two yards. It is now thought that Cadosh had been mere feet away from Jack the Ripper committing one of his terrible crimes.

27.  Although testimony of witnesses placed the time of death at 5:30 a.m., the police surgeon, Dr George Bagster Phillips, estimated it as 4:30 a.m. Although we will never know for sure, the witness reports may be the more likely, as Victorian methods for estimating time of death were particularly crude.

28.   Chapman's throat had been cut from left to right in the same manner as Mary Ann Nichols, the first victim. She had however also been disembowelled, with her intestines gruesomely pulled out of her abdomen and strung across each of her shoulders. It was later found at her autopsy that part of her uterus was missing. As her tongue and face were swollen, investigators believed she had been strangled with a handkerchief before her throat was slit.

29.   It was deduced that Annie had been murdered at the place she was found, as there was no blood trail leading to the body. It was suggested by the police surgeon that the killer would have required medical knowledge to remove the part of the uterus he did in one swipe of the 6 to 8 inch knife he (or she) used; although this way of thinking was disputed by other experts, it helped form the basis of a number of theories as to who the killer was which continue being debated to this day.

30.   At the family's request, Annie's funeral was carried out in secret on the 14th of September 1888 at 9 a.m. She was buried in a public grave, number 78 in square 148 which no longer exists today as it has been buried over, space being so limited in London's cemeteries.

*Dr Phillips Examining the Body of Annie Chapman*

# Elizabeth Stride

31. Elizabeth, a Swedish farmer's daughter, was born on the 27th of November 1843 and was the third of Jack the Ripper's known murder victims.

32. She was five feet two inches tall with light grey eyes, a pale complexion and curly dark brown hair.

33. Elizabeth began working as a prostitute in her earlier years in Sweden – she was known to the police in Gothenburg as a street worker when she was in her early twenties, having twice been treated for sexually transmitted diseases. Moving to London in 1866 with a family as their domestic servant, she met (and three years later married) John Thomas Stride, a man thirteen years her senior.

34. John and Elizabeth did not have children together, although she made up fanciful stories of tragedy that she told acquaintances, such as two of nine children she had borne were drowned in a tragic riverboat accident. During her years in London she appeared in front of magistrates a number of times for being drunk and disorderly – at the time giving her name as Anne Fitzgerald. it is believed that she continued her work as a prostitute throughout her time in London.

35. At 12:35 a.m. on the 30th of September 1888, a policeman, PC William Smith, saw Elizabeth opposite a predominantly Jewish social club at 40 Berner Street. She was with a man wearing a hard felt

hat and carrying a package around 45 centimetres long. A witness named Israel Schwartz reports he saw her ten minutes later being attacked and thrown to the ground by a man close to the social club in a location called Dutfield's Yard. However another witness, James Brown, reports seeing her in the adjacent street rejecting the advanced of a stoutish man. The police admitted that both reports could be true as there was time for her to have met the man in the adjacent street before returning to the area close to the yard.

36. At 1 a.m., the steward of the club, Louis Diemschutz, drove into Dutfield's yard on his pony and cart. The horse panicked and Diemschutz alighted to investigate. Striking a match in the pitch blackness, he saw to his horror Elizabeth's body, blood still gushing from a neck wound, suggesting the poor woman had been killed just moments before he arrived. Other members of the club who had passed the yard ten minutes earlier, and therefore an extremely recent time of death could be considered highly likely.

37. Whereas the other confirmed victims of Jack the Ripper had been mutilated, especially across the abdomen, the only wound Elizabeth's body had was the slit to the throat – however this was in the characteristic Ripper style. Terrifyingly for Diemschutz, he came to the conclusion that Jack the Ripper was still in the yard when he discovered the body, and he had stopped him in the middle of his latest frenzied attack.

38. A post mortem found that Elizabeth had been pulled backwards onto the ground by her neckerchief before having her throat slashed – a swift cut from left to right as expected from Jack's terrible hand. The poor wretch had been pinned to the ground during the Ripper's attack which had caused bruising to her chest.

39. An intriguing clue as to the Ripper's identity was proffered by one witness, a grocer who says he sold some grapes to Elizabeth who was accompanied by a man he believed to be her murderer. Although the pathologist did not find any grapes in the contents of the victim's stomach, detectives did find a grape stalk in the yard where her life came to an end. The man who accompanied Stride to buy the fruit was between 25 and 30, slightly taller than her, and wearing a felt hat.

40. On Saturday the 6th of October 1888, Elizabeth Stride was buried at the East London Cemetery in grave number 15509, square 37. Some historians have since cast doubt on whether she was the ripper's third victim; the blade used was most likely shorter than the one used on the other victims (according to elementary forensic judgement of the day), it was the only murder to occur *south* of the Whitechapel Road, and that the body was unmutilated. Only the Ripper himself would ever know the truth.

| Registration District | | | Saint George in the East |
|---|---|---|---|

1888. Death in the Sub-district of St. George North in the County of Middlesex

| No | When and where died | Name and surname | Sex | Age | Occupation | Cause of death | Signature, description, and residence of informant | When registered | Signature of registrar |
|---|---|---|---|---|---|---|---|---|---|
| 479 | Thirtieth September 1888 In a yard at the side of no 40 Berner Street St. George | Elizabeth STRIDE | Female | 45 years | Widow of John Thomas STRIDE Carpenter | Violent Haemorrhage from severance of blood vessels in the neck by a sharp instrument. Murder against some person or persons unknown. Post mortem | Certificate received from Wynne E. Baxter Coroner for London W. 23rd October 1888 | Twenty fourth October 1888 | Registrar |

*Elizabeth Stride's Death Certificate*

# Catherine Eddowes

41.    Catherine, one of ten children of parents George and Catherine Eddowes, was born on the 14th of April 1842. She is considered to be the fourth victim of Jack the Ripper.

42.    She was five feet tall with hazel eyes, dark auburn hair and sported a tattoo on her left forearm that read *TC* – these letters stood for Thomas Conway, an ex-soldier Catherine had three children with.

43.    Catherine became a drunk after bearing her third child (although it is likely she showed alcoholic tendencies throughout her adult life). Splitting from Conway in 1880 she took up home with a man called John Kelly, living in a notorious criminal slum in Dean Street. Here she took up casual prostitution to pay her rent, unable to hold down any other meaningful form of employment.

44.    A policeman, PC Louis Robinson, found Eddowes lying drunk on Aldgate High Street at dusk on Saturday the 29th of September 1888. He took her into custody at Bishopsgate Police Station, where she could only mutter 'nothing' in answer to the question of her name. A few hours later, at 1 a.m. on the morning of the 30th of September, she had sobered up enough to give a different (but more coherent) name, this time Mary Ann Kelly, and said she lived at 6 Fashion Street. She was released,

although on leaving the station she was seen turning left towards Aldgate, rather than turning right, the more direct route to her *actual* home.

45. At 1:35 a.m. three witnesses claim to have seen Catherine talking with a man at the entrance of Church Passage. One of these, Joseph Lawende, provided a description of the man, saying he sported a fair moustache, wore a peaked cloth cap and was clothed in a navy jacket and red scarf. However, the chief inspector on the case felt that the witnesses may not have seen Eddowes herself, as the identification relied purely on the fact that the woman they saw was wearing black, which wasn't exactly uncommon at the time.

46. Ten minutes after this alleged last sighting, Catherine's mutilated body was found in the south-west corner of Mitre Square, the road at the end of Church Passage. Her throat had been cut and her face grossly disfigured. Her intestines had been mostly pulled out of her body and were thrown over her right shoulder. The entrails themselves were smeared with faecal matter. One piece, around 60cm long, had been totally separated and placed deliberately between the woman's torso and left arm. Her right ear had also been cut in two places. Finally, it was later discovered that Eddowes's left kidney had been totally removed from her corpse; the organ itself would have been of no use to anyone – an additional element of insanity in this senseless, brutal murder.

47. The eagle-eyed reader will spot that the date of Eddowes's killing is the same as that of Elizabeth Stride. This is known by students of the Ripper's crimes as the *double event*; this is another reason why doubt is cast on Stride being a *true* victim of Jack... however, others argue that the case for her is strengthened; it would seem that his lust was not satisfied with his first killing, having been interrupted prior to beginning the mutilations. He therefore continued to prowl for a second victim, coming across the unfortunate Eddowes.

48. Because Catherine's body was found within the limits of the City of London – actually only a one-mile square patch of land in the middle of *Greater London* – the City of London Police joined the investigation. Their officers were often better trained and had more specialist skills than the normal beat bobbies, and therefore it was now hoped that the two forces working together would make progress on the case.

49. A grizzly parcel was received by the police on the 16th of October. The two things it contained were a letter (now referred to as the 'From Hell' letter, discussed elsewhere in this book) and half a human kidney, purporting to be part of the one removed from Catherine's body at the time of her death. The other half, according to whoever had sent the package, had been fried and eaten. One source tells us that the kidney was almost certainly from Eddowes's body (meaning the accompanying letter was not a hoax) as not only did the length of the renal artery left attached to this kidney match the missing length

of the artery in the body, but also both this kidney and the unmolested one showed signs of Bright's disease. However, other sources dispute this tale, suggesting police records note it was likely to be a prank by medical students. As with much to do with the Ripper's antics, we shall most likely never know which story to believe.

50. On the 8th of October, Catherine was laid to rest in an elm coffin in the City of London Cemetery, in grave 49336, square 318. Her body has since been moved close to the cemetery's memorial bed number 1849, and it was only in 1966 that the authorities marked the new spot with a plaque dedicated to the poor woman's memory.

CERTIFIED COPY OF AN ENTRY OF DEATH

| | REGISTRATION DISTRICT | | | | | | | | |
|---|---|---|---|---|---|---|---|---|---|
| 1888 | DEATH in the Sub-district of | | | Londion City | | | in the City of London | | |
| No. | When and where died | Name and surname | Sex | Age | Occupation | Cause of death | Signature, description, and residence of informant | When registered | Signature of registrar |
| 256 | 30th September 1888 found dead Church Passage Mitre Square | Catherine Eddowes | Female | 43 years | supposed single woman | Homicide from the ill usage of the neck by being cut by a person or persons unknown and shock from loss of blood from the wound. Wilful murder against some person or persons unknown | Certificate received from Thos. Langham Coroner for London held an inquest held 4th and 11th October 1888 | Thirteenth day of October 1888 | Fullom Registrar |

*Death Certificate of Catherine Eddowes*

# Mary Jane Kelly

51. Mary, born in 1863 and daughter of iron Worker John Kelly, is considered to be the fifth and final victim of Jack the Ripper.

52. We do not have as much certainty on Mary's background today as we'd like; no records of her early life can be found. However, based on what information she told friends and lovers (which could of course have been embellished but we shall take at face value as there is nothing to dispute it), Mary was born in Limerick, Ireland before moving to Wales at a young age. She said she had seven brothers and at least one sister, and that one of her brothers was in the Scots Guard. Two that knew her in fact said she was from a very well-to-do background, a scholar and an artist, however her most recent partner disagreed, saying that she couldn't even read.

53. After her husband, a coal miner named Davies (who married Mary when she was just 16) was killed in an explosion, Mary moved in with her cousin and began her career as a prostitute. It is thought that as an attractive lady Mary first found well-paid work in an upmarket West end brothel – even moving briefly to France with a rich client. However, taking to drink and perhaps falling in with the wrong men, she gravitated towards life in the poorer East end of the city.

54. Mary had a number of Nicknames – Fair Emma, Ginger and Black Mary or Dark Mary. Any of these could have related to the colour of her hair, the true shade of which has not been recorded, however the latter is thought to refer to her temper. After drinking she would sing Irish songs in good spirits, but then would often soon turn abusive, even to those close to her.

55. The night of the 8th of November and the early hours of the 9th were the last time Kelly was seen alive. Her on-off lover Joseph Barnett left her lodgings between 7 and 8pm on the 8th, and at that point Mary was in the company of a friend, Maria Harvey. Approaching midnight, a fellow prostitute from another room within the same lodging house reported seeing Mary Jane return to her room (having apparently gone out into the night after Barnett had left) in a drunk state and accompanied by a stout ginger-haired man who was sporting a bowler hat. At 1 a.m. Kelly was still singing, however – according to the woman who lived in the room above – it had stopped by 1:30am on the 9th.

56. One witness, George Hutchinson, gave the police a statement which told how he saw Kelly with a Jewish-looking man at around 2:00 a.m. the same night, however although the police were initially interested in this sighting it is thought they later discounted it as unreliable.

57. On the morning of the 9th, Mary Jane's landlord sent an ex-solider named Thomas Bowyer round to her lodgings to collect six weeks of back rent. Receiving no response after he knocked on the door at 10:45 a.m., he reached through a crack in the window, pushed the coat hanging there aside (which was being used as a temporary curtain) and saw the horrifying sight of a mutilated corpse. The ripper had struck again.

58. Mary Jane's abdomen and thighs had been cut open, with all the skin removed from them. Her intestines and internal organs had been wholly removed and her breasts completely cut off. There were a number of vicious, jagged wounds in her arms and the poor woman's face had been hacked apart so terribly that her features were no longer recognisable. The skin had been cut from all around her neck so that bone was visible from all angles. Kelly's uterus, kidneys and one breast were placed under her head as some kind of gruesome pillow, whereas another breast lie at one of her feet, alongside her liver. The spleen was placed by the left side of the body and the intestines to the right. The flaps of skin which had previously covered her thighs and abdomen had been situated on a nearby table. Across the entire corpse, a massive number of other cuts and slices had been made. Investigators concluded that – as with the ripper's other victims – Kelly had been killed by a left/right slash to her throat, and the further wounds inflicted after death; it is believed that the mutilations would have taken two full hours. A post-mortem

concluded that death occurred between the hours of 1:00 a.m. and 8:00 a.m., although earlier was more likely.

59. Since the occurrences of that terrible year in Whitechapel, some have suggested that Mary Jane was not in fact a victim of the ripper, but was killed by Barnett in a jealous rage, and that after doing so he made it look like a ripper murder. However, the police questioned the man at length after the murder, and were satisfied enough not to charge him.

60. Mary Jane was buried at St Patrick's Roman Catholic Cemetery in Leytonstone on the 19th of November. Her grave, which was reclaimed 60 years later, was in plot 10 and was number 66, row 66.

**Registration District** Whitechapel

1888. **Death in the Sub-district of** Spitalfields **in the** County of **Middlesex**

| No. | When and where died | Name and surname | Sex | Age | Occupation | Cause of death | Signature, description, and residence of informant | When registered | Signature of registrar |
|-----|---------------------|------------------|-----|-----|------------|----------------|-----------------------------------------------------|------------------|-------------------------|
| 526 | 9th November 1888 13 Millers Court Dorset Street Christchurch | Marie Jeanette KELLY otherwise DAVIES | Female | about 25 years | Prostitute | Exsanguination through carotid artery Wilful murder against some person or persons unknown Verdict | Certificate received from Roderick MacDonald Coroner for Middlesex Inquest held 12th November | November W. Edwards 1888 | Registrar |

*Death Certificate of Mary Jane Kelly*

# Letters

61.  On the 27th of September 1888, almost three weeks
     after the ripper's second murder, the Central
     News Agency received a letter which was initially
     believed to be a hoax; despite this, it *was* certainly
     the source of the name Jack the Ripper, being the
     earliest written document which uses the name.
     The letter, known to students of the case as the
     'Dear Boss' letter read thusly: *Dear Boss, I keep on*
     *hearing the police have caught me but they wont fix*
     *me just yet. I have laughed when they look so clever*
     *and talk about being on the right track. That joke*
     *about Leather Apron gave me real fits. I am down*
     *on whores and I shant quit ripping them till I do get*
     *buckled. Grand work the last job was. I gave the lady*
     *no time to squeal. How can they catch me now. I love*
     *my work and want to start again. You will soon hear*
     *of me with my funny little games. I saved some of the*
     *proper red stuff in a ginger beer bottle over the last*
     *job to write with but it went thick like glue and I cant*
     *use it. Red ink is fit enough I hope ha. ha. The next*
     *job I do I shall clip the ladys ears off and send to the*
     *police officers just for jolly wouldn't you. Keep this*
     *letter back till I do a bit more work, then give it out*
     *straight. My knife's so nice and sharp I want to get to*
     *work right away if I get a chance. Good Luck.*

62.  Three days later however, the letter was re-
     evaluated. The promise in the letter to 'clip the lady's
     ears off' was relevant to the mutilation of Catherine
     Eddowes which occurred on the 30th of September,

and therefore the police requested it be published in the newspapers in the hope that someone would recognise the handwriting.

63.   On the 1st of October, just one day after the 'double event' – and before details of it were made public – the News Agency received another missive, now known as the 'Saucy Jacky' postcard. The handwriting was similar to the previous letter and referenced details the were certainly not known by outsiders to the case at the time. Was this proof that it was from that Ripper's own hand? It read as follows: *I was not codding dear old Boss when I gave you the tip, you'll hear about Saucy Jacky's work tomorrow double event this time number one squealed a bit couldn't finish straight off. ha not the time to get ears for police. thanks for keeping last letter back till I got to work again. Jack the Ripper*

64.   On the 6th of the same month, another letter purporting to be from the Ripper was received by the offices of a local newspaper and is thought to have been intended for one of the witnesses who had given a description of who they believed to be the killer. After much study, this letter is not believed to be genuine, and was most likely the scrawlings of a hoaxer. it read: *You though your-self very clever I reckon when you informed the police. But you made a mistake if you though I dident see you. Now I known you know me and I see your little game, and I mean to finish you and send your ears to your wife if you show this to the police or help them if you do I will*

*finish you. It no use your trying to get out of my way. Because I have you when you dont expect it and I keep my word as you soon see and rip you up. Yours truly Jack the Ripper. PS You see I know your address*

65. Ten days later, George Lusk, the president of the Whitechapel Vigilance Committee (the neighbourhood watch of the day) received a grizzly package. It contained a human kidney preserved in wine along with a letter, now known as the 'From Hell' letter. Although the kidney appeared to be very similar to that removed from Catherine Eddowes, technology at the time prevented this from being conclusively proven. It read: *From hell. Mr Lusk, Sor I send you half the Kidne I took from one woman and prasarved it for you tother piece I fried and ate it was very nise. I may send you the bloody knif that took it out if you only wate a whil longer. Signed. Catch me when you can Mishter Lusk*

66. A further letter, of which we do not have an exact date of delivery and which was not believed to be genuine read as follows: *Beware I shall be at work on the 1st and 2nd inst. in the Minories at 12 midnight and I give the authorities a good chance but there is never a policeman near when I am at work. Yours Jack the Ripper.*

67. Yet another letter (again with no confirmed date of delivery on file) even purported to reveal the street on which the perpetrator of the murders lived. Most – but not all – researchers believe this also to be a

hoax. It read: *What fools the police are. I even give them the name of the street where I am living. Prince William Street.*

68. Dr Openshaw, the surgeon who had inspected the kidney sent alongside the From Hell letter received a communique himself on the 29th of October. Again, it is not thought to be from the murderer's hand, although – as with everything ripper related – we cannot be sure. This one read: *Old boss you was rite it was the left kidny i was goin to hoperate agin close to you ospitle just as i was going to dror mi nife along of er bloomin throte them cusses of coppers spoilt the game but i guess i wil be on the jobn soon and will send you another bit of innerds. Jack the Ripper. O have you seen the devle with his mikerscope and scalpul a-lookin at a kidney with a slide cocked up.*

69. Amazingly, only relatively recently (in 1988 in fact) a further letter was found in a sealed report envelope from the time held in the Public Records Office. Whereas it could well be genuine, some have dismissed it as a recent hoax rather than one from the time. It read: *17th Sept 1888. Dear Boss. So now they say I am a Yid when will they lern Dear old Boss! You an me know the truth dont we. Lusk can look forever hell never find me but I am rite under his nose all the time. I watch them looking for me an it gives me fits ha ha I love my work an I shant stop until I get buckled and even then watch out for your old pal Jacky. Catch me if you Can. Jack the Ripper. Sorry about the blood still messy from the last one. What a pretty necklace I gave her.*

70. Throughout the case, many other (fairly obviously) hoax letters were sent to the police – although not all were recorded or survive to this day. Often these were in the form of verse. Here is just one: *Eight little whores, with no hope of heaven, Gladstone may save one, then there'll be seven. Seven little whores beggin for a shilling, One stays in Henage Court, then there's a killing. Six little whores, glad to be alive, One sidles up to Jack, then there are five. Four and whore rhyme aright, So do three and me, I'll set the town alight. Ere there are two. Two little whores, shivering with fright, Seek a cosy doorway in the middle of the night. Jack's knife flashes, then there's but one, And the last one's the ripest for Jack's idea of fun.*

25. Sept. 1988.

Dear Boss

I keep on hearing the police
have caught me. but they wont fix
me just yet. I have laughed when
they look so clever and talk about
being on the right track. That joke
about Leather apron gave me real
fits. I am down on whores and
I shant quit ripping them till I
do get buckled. Grand work the last
job was. I gave the lady no time to
squeal. How can they catch me now.
I love my work and want to start
again. You will soon hear of me
with my funny little games. I
saved some of the proper red stuff in
a ginger beer bottle over the last job
to write with but it went thick
like glue and I cant use it. Red
ink is fit enough I hope ha. ha.
The next job I do I shall clip
the ladys ears off and send to the

*The First Page of the 'Dear Boss' Letter*

police officers just for jolly wouldnt you. Keep this letter back till I do a bit more work. then give it out straight My knife's so nice and sharp I want to get to work right away if I get a chance. Good luck.

yours truly

Jack the Ripper

Dont mind me giving the trade name

wasnt good enough to post this before I got all the red ink off my hands curse it No luck yet. They say I'm a doctor now ha ha

The Second Page of the 'Dear Boss' Letter

# Interesting Facts

71.   There is no waxwork of Jack the Ripper in London's Madame Tussauds, as the museum has a policy of not having models of figures of whom we do not know the true depiction. Jack is represented therefore by a shadow.

72.   In a poll by BBC's *History* Magazine, Jack was voted the worst Briton of all time.

73.   The rumour that Jack the Ripper was left-handed was started by a speculative comment by Dr Henry Llewllyn, the surgeon who had attended the scene of the first murder. However, he later cast doubt on his own though but the belief had already cemented itself in the public consciousness.

74.   When the first murder was reported, rumours circulated that it had been committed by a man called 'leather apron', which was sadly an invention of the media, using Jewish stereotypes at the time (there were racial tensions due to immigration from a number of ethnic groups in London at the time). A local Polish Jew called John Pizer was also known as 'Leather Apron' (relating to his trade of making leather footwear) and was arrested at the time despite there being absolutely no evidence against him. After being released when his alibis were confirmed, he successfully sued a newspaper who had named him as the murderer.

75.   The acting commissioner of the City Police was a man called Major Henry Smith. Twenty years after the events, he published a memoir however it is well-known for having been embellished for dramatic effect. One particular comment he made in his book was that medical students polished farthings to look like sovereigns (coins of a higher value); as at the inquest of Annie Chapman it was mentioned that two farthings had been found on her body, Smith suggested the culprit must therefore have been a medical student. Ignoring the huge gaps in the logic, the price of a prostitute in the east end of London was a great deal less than one sovereign so his theory, deduction and its importance to the case do not ring true.

76.   In the early hours of September 30th 1888 Jack unusually committed two murders within the space of an hour – known as the double event. The two women whose lives were brutally taken were Elizabeth Stride and Catherine Eddowes. Some would say Jack was clever in that *if* he committed these two murders he did so within two different boroughs; meaning the case now fell under two different police jurisdictions; City Police and the Metropolitan. This caused quite a stir given that until now the Metropolitan Police had had full control.

77.   That same morning, Police in Whitechapel came across a bloodied strip of clothing, belonging to the apron Catherine Eddowes (The second victim in the double event) had been wearing but they also found

some chalk writing on a wall. No one is certain of the exact words as Commissioner Sir Charles Warren ordered the writing be removed before photographers arrived at the scene (later fuelling rumours of a police cover up and even protection for Jack from on high). However, he did record the note on a piece of paper reading: *The Juwes are the men who will not be blamed for nothing.* Although two other police officers at the scene claimed the writing contained an extra *not*, reading: *The Juwes are **not** the men who will not be blamed for nothing.* The *official* reasons given for removing the writing were to avoid any violence and prevent a possible riot.

78. The Ten Bells pub situated on the corner of commercial Street and Fournier Street still stands today and was known to a few of the Ripper victims; mainly Annie Chapman and Mary Jane Kelly, it is thought that Annie drank at the pub shortly before her murder. Decades later, between 1976 and 1988 the pub's name was distastefully changed to The Jack the Ripper and began selling memorabilia relating to the horrific murders. The brewery ordered that the pub be changed back to its original name after a long campaign by Reclaim the Night demanded the brutal murder of women should not be commemorated in such a fashion.

79. Recently, it was claimed by a former murder squad detective with Befordshire Police that the entire Jack the Ripper case had been a hoax! The suggestion was that The persona of the Ripper was just dreamed up by a drunken journalist called Thomas Bulling who wrote the 'From Hell' letter pretending to be Jack so he could obtain a scoop.

80. It has been reported that ghosts of victims – and possibly even Jack himself – have been seen in the various locations connected with the case. Anyone particularly interested in paranormal phenomena may wish to visit the Ten Bells pub, where a number of encounters with ghostly Victorian figures have been reported.

BLIND-MAN'S BUFF.

*[As played by the Police.]*

"TURN ROUND THREE TIMES,
AND CATCH WHOM YOU MAY!"

*Cartoon Criticising the Police Investigation*

# Clues to the Ripper's Identity

*For more than 125 years, people have attempted to discover the Ripper's true identity, using a number of clues which are considered highly important to the case. Studying these, perhaps you can succeed where others have failed?*

81. **He was skilled with a blade.** Although there are arguments on both sides of this point, many experts agree that Jack must have had at least some medical knowledge when he committed his crimes – whether this had come from animals or humans of course is not known. On balance it is thought that the way he removed certain organs displayed a level of knowledge a normal member of the public would not have had.

82. **He was uneducated.** This seems to contradict the first point, although this is not necessarily the case, although it perhaps points more to someone used to working with animals than with the human body.

83. **He may have had protection from the Masons or other high-standing members of society.** There was a fair amount of *apparent* incompetence from the metropolitan police, certainly in the early stages of the case. A common suggestion is that various elements of the investigation were covered up or thwarted by senior figures, whether within the force or amongst those who commanded some kind of influence over it – possibly even royal.

84. **He had a hatred of prostitutes.** This should be fairly clear – the five 'canonical' murders were all actively working prostitutes. Of course, it could be argued that the nature of their work meant that prostitution was the most likely occupation for victims (walking the streets on dark nights), however plenty of other jobs required individuals to be out during the small hours at that time in London, so it does seem that Jack deliberately targeted those who earned their living from sex.

85. **He was insane.** Again, a fairly logical deduction. It is one thing to murder, but another to mutilate a dead body afterwards. Jack clearly revelled in the latter, certainly if one counts Mary Jane Kelly as a definite Ripper victim.

86. **He is thought to have stopped killing after the 8th of November.** Most researchers believe that although other murders occurred in the area, his final killing was that of Mary Jane Kelly. The question must therefore be asked as to why he stopped. Was he imprisoned for another offence? Was he found out and secretly punished, locked away in a mental asylum or even warned not to do it again by those who knew his true identity? Did he die? Did he move abroad? This is certainly one of the key elements to discovering jack's true identity.

87. **He was local to Whitechapel.** Analysis of the killings point to the fact the killer knew the area – and some (possibly even all) of the victims personally. On the night of the double event he seems to have escaped the scene of the first crime calmly, perhaps even blending into a crowd – not something one would expect of an outsider who would almost certainly look out of place.

88. **He took risks.** In every single one of the killings – even the last which was conducted inside – Jack could have been discovered carrying out his awful rituals by any number of people; think of the body slumping against the fence, of being disturbed in the alleyway, of a neighbour checking everything was alright... but Jack didn't care. Yet he didn't carry the attacks out in full view of the public either.

89. **Which description to believe?** Was he tall and foreign? Did he look 'Jewish'? Was he ginger? Did he wear a cape? A bowler hat? Almost every possible witness description of potential Jack the Ripper sightings seem to disagree. Of course, the question must be asked was every killing committed by a different individual – or did he have multiple accomplices? We must, however, place our faith in the investigators of the day (and since) who agree that one man killed these five women for sure.

90. **He gave gifts to the victims.** Perhaps a key insight into his modus operandi. Eddowes was found carrying a red cigarette case that was worth more than she could have realistically afforded that night. Mary Jane Kelly was seen by one witness being given a red handkerchief, possibly of expensive material. Elizabeth Stride was seen with a man purchasing grapes, an expensive commodity. It is speculated therefore that Jack could have lured his victims out late at night and to a secluded area by meeting them *earlier on that day* and buttering them up with an expensive token. The question must therefore be asked: do these gifts give us any clues as to his actual identity? He certainly couldn't have been a poor man.

*The message on the wall - as recorded in police files*

# Suspects

*In a time before forensic science and finger printing existed tracking down a murderer wouldn't have been the easiest of jobs, unless you were lucky enough to catch them in the act. Due to this and the fact Jack the Ripper was never caught there was lots of speculation as to who this gruesome murderer really was. With more than one hundred individuals linked to the Ripper's identity over the years it would be hard (and a little tedious) to supply information for all of them. However, here are details of a a number of interesting suspects that have been proposed over the years. Some seem likely, others outlandish. However, it must be stressed that all are purely speculative...*

91.  Perhaps the most famous and well-known of all the potential suspects is Prince Albert Victor Christian Edward... although these allegations came years after the murders had ceased and were supposedly rubbished by a number of people (and also ignored the fact that he had alibis for the murders, although there *could* have been a cover-up). The first written reference to Albert as a suspect was in Philippe Jullian's biography of Albert's father, Edward VII. Only a passing reference to a rumour that Albert being Jack the Ripper was made, and in fact no dates nor sources were quoted. Despite this, the possibility that a royal was in fact the Ripper caught the people's imagination and decades later became firmly cemented in the public consciousness. We then move further down the rumour mill to 1970 when a Dr Thomas E. A. Stowell published an

article in *The Criminologist* which actually revealed a reason as to why *he* suspected Prince Albert – the man had been driven mad by Syphilis. Strangely, Stowell later denied implying that Albert had been the Ripper however! Stowell's papers were later burned by his son after he'd "made certain they contained nothing of any importance" meaning if he had uncovered any actual evidence that *could* prove Albert was responsible, it was now lost to history.

92. It wasn't just Stowell who named Albert as the Ripper though; in a book called *Prince Jack* by Frank Spiering, Albert is clearly named as the infamous murderer. Spiering claimed to have found a copy of the medical notes of Sir William Gull, Prince Albert's doctor, which included a report that he had hypnotized Albert and watched on in horror as he acted out the murders. Again, no evidence of these papers remain. Another modern day theory has suggested that Prince Albert had secretly married and fathered a child with a shop assistant and anyone outside his immediate circle that found out was murdered.

93. Interestingly, Sir William Gull is our next suspect. Some believe Gull *himself* carried out the murders, possibly with an accomplice. Others believe he was well aware that Prince Albert was the Ripper and that they may have even worked together. Gull is named as a potential suspect in a great number of books and films, and is certainly a popular choice for the Ripper's identity. Could these gruesome and brutal murders have been his doing?

94. A man named George Hutchinson is also high on the list. On the 12th of November 1888 he entered a London police station claiming that three days previously he had watched the room in which Mary Jane Kelly was murdered, after seeing her with a suspicious looking man. His description was particularly detailed – especially given that this was during the late hours and light was not on his side. His statement was questioned among senior police (although after an interview, Inspector Frank Abberline believed his account to be truthful). However, Robert Anderson, head of CID, later said that the only witness he believed was Jewish. Although we have no record of who this referred to, we know Hutchinson was not – and therefore that the police at the time ultimately concluded that his statement was not true. Some therefore think that perhaps Hutchinson *himself* was the Ripper, trying to throw the police off the scent. Others believe he may have just been an attention seeker hoping to sell his story. The possibility of course does remain that he was a *genuine* witness who just wasn't taken seriously...

95. An unusual and unlikely suspect is that of Charles Dodgson... better known as Lewis Carroll, author of the much loved book *Alice's Adventures in Wonderland*. The rather outlandish theory belongs to author Richard Wallace and is based on a number of anagrams derived from passages within two of Carroll's works, *The Nursery of Alice* and *Alice's Adventures in Wonderland*. Most people have

dismissed this theory, stating it has some serious logical flaws and that the same method can be applied to any number of works written in English, given enough time and effort.

96. Another potential suspect was Montague John Druitt whose body was found floating in the Thames a little over a month after the last murder took place. The only *real* link connecting him to the murders is the coincidental timing of his death. It is thought that he may have lain dead in the river for a few weeks (due to the level of decomposition of his body, which had been held underwater by stones in his pocket) which means that he could well have died shortly after the last of the five murders, explaining why (if he was the killer) they stopped so suddenly. Strangely, police at the time thought the stones in his pockets indicated suicide, whereas one perhaps would think this is more of a sign of murder. A cover-up from on high perhaps? Also, some suggest that because Druitt's family had suffered from mental health problems, then if *he* also did then he may have been insane enough to be the ripper – yet intriguingly at the time the police used this as a reason to *discount* him as a suspect. Regardless of these additional mysteries, one thing that doesn't tie up is the accepted 'fact' that the Ripper was local to Whitechapel; Druitt lived in Kent.

97.  John Pizer was a Jewish man working as a bootmaker who went by the nickname 'Leather Apron'. On the 10th of September he was arrested, with police sergeant William Thicke believing he had previously committed a number of minor assaults on prostitutes. At the time many believed him to be behind the Whitechapel murders, certainly not helped by the rumour that the first murder was committed by someone also named Leather Apron. However, an investigating officer at the time stated there was no evidence against him at all (of course, there is no *real* evidence against any suspect on this list) and Pizer was cleared when he provided alibis (one of them a police officer!) for two of the murders.

98.  Sir Arthur Conan Doyle and William Stuart took a different approach to the suspect and devised the theory that the murderer may have in fact been a female who posed as a midwife, therefore gaining the trust of women more easily and being able to sport bloodied clothing without raising suspicion. The only person to fit this profile even vaguely was Mary Pearcey, who in October 1890 murdered both her lover's wife and child – although there is no evidence to suggest she was actually a midwife. It should be noted that recently, DNA taken from the letters widely considered to be from the 'real' killer was tested for gender, but the results were inconclusive, so we cannot rule out the possibility of a female killer – of course, we are not *certain* whether the letters to the police even came from the murderer. So why haven't more people considered

the fact that *he* may have actually been a *she*? Perhaps even in today's world it is still considered quite rare for a woman to become a single handed serial killer... plus it must have taken a huge amount of strength to kill these women; something a woman back then was unlikely to have had.

99. A man born in Poland with the name Seweryn Antonowicz Kłosowski moved to London shortly before the Ripper murders. He worked as a barber in Whitechapel at the time of the killings and apparently was Inspector Frederick Abberline's favoured suspect. Although there was no physical evidence to link him to the case, a few years later he changed his name to George Chapman and then murdered three of his wives – crimes he was in fact hanged for in 1903. This perhaps seems to strengthen the case against him, however it should be noted that the method of dispatch he chose was poisoning – surely the Ripper wouldn't have 'softened' his approach?

100. Lastly, we will mention Joseph Barnett, friend of Mary Jane Kelly, the final victim. He was questioned in detail when her body was found, and police at the time suspected he may have killed her – although, of course, this was never proven. Did Barnett kill Kelly and make it look like a ripper murder? Or was Barnett responsible for *all* of the killings, only stopping because the police got too close? There are a number of links which cannot be ignored. Barnett's physical description matches that given by more than one witness statement. Ginger beer

bottles were found in his apartment (note the passage from the 'Dear Boss' letter which says *saved some of the proper red stuff in a **ginger beer bottle** over the last job to write with).* He was experienced with a knife, as his job involved gutting fish. He had a speech impediment which, according to current FBI theories, would have frustrated him possibly to the level of insanity, and finally he is likely to have held a key to Kelly's lodgings, solving the mystery of how her door was locked when her body was found inside.

*Sir William Gull, One of the Many Jack the Ripper Suspects*

# And Finally...

101. A number of online resources exist that will give any Ripper aficionado much more information than this book can provide. One site that is certainly worth spending a great deal of time on is *Casebook: Jack the Ripper* which can be found at www.casebook.org

Also from Jack Goldstein and Frankie Taylor

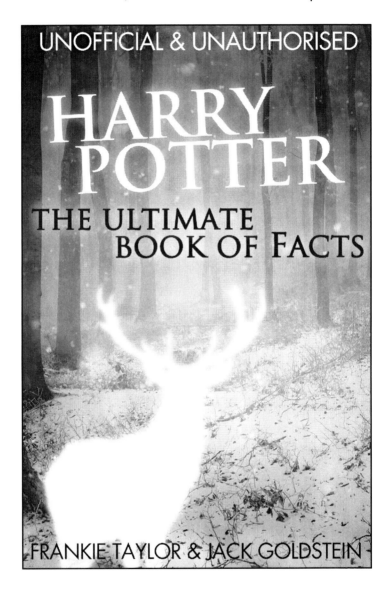

UNOFFICIAL & UNAUTHORISED

HARRY POTTER

THE ULTIMATE BOOK OF FACTS

FRANKIE TAYLOR & JACK GOLDSTEIN

Lightning Source UK Ltd.
Milton Keynes UK
UKOW04f1856260116

267187UK00001B/3/P